Praise

I0458391

When I Go West

William Sheldon's *When I Go West: New and Selected Poems* invites us right in with "The world says hello and makes it promise," then makes good on that promise. With keen observation of the life force in motion, Sheldon shows us how to hone our own awareness of the tiny and not-so-tiny stories roaring, flying, or rising all around us, from fingernail moons to a better heaven to " . . . a sky I love each time I see it, no matter/ its form." This whole book is imbued with the attention such love summons for the here and now. "'I love this world,'" he writes in "Yes, I Said Perfect," reminding us of the realest news, as free and available as our breath and the wind. This collection of his considerably vivid, jaunty, surprising, and honest poems is full of lanterns, maps, gardens, and river ways that help us see not just the world, but the promise that "There is only love / and its absence."

> —Caryn Mirriam-Goldberg, Poet Laureate of Kansas 2009-13, *The Magic Eye: A Story of Saving a Life and a Place in the Age of Anxiety*

When I Go West is a beautiful collection of poems that sees life's daily promise for small beauties. Sheldon is definitely a writer of place and renders the Kansas landscape with precision, but the pleasures of a yard are made universal. Sheldon distills images we see most days, but he makes us stop glancing at the world and really look—at every tender morning, at every bird feeder, at every ripening tomato. These poems remind me of the awe that resides in quiet moments is a primer on how to love this world.

> —Traci Brimhall, Poet Laureate of Kansas 2023-2026, *Love Prodigal*

William Sheldon has secrets to share, if you'll stop and hear his gentle voice echo across the plains. It's far from a hard sell. In fact, there's an easy welcome waiting, as if he asked you to spend the day with him, discovering all he knows about the natural world and each wonder he finds there. In this splendid collection, *When I Go West: New and Selected Poems*, the poet cradles us under his wing and takes flight, revealing what exists below—a teeming landscape of heartbreak and beauty.

> —Bart Edelman, *This Body Is Never at Rest, New and Selected Poems 1993–2023*

Rain Comes Riding

Rain Comes Riding details the poet's passion for his chosen place and time. He is a poet who fully embraces the contradictions of simulated realities existing, fragmented and dislocated, in a timeless universe of bluestem grass. [This book] shows him creating a new genre, a ballad for new times in an ancient place.

> —Denise Low, Poet Laureate of Kansas Emeritus, *House of Grace, House of Blood: Poems*

Rain Comes Riding, steeped in history and family, in an intimacy of place and sometimes a wry sense of humor, is the record of a career in which the world and the word have been lovingly wedded.

> —Albert Goldbarth, National Book Critics Circle Award winner, *Ludd Light*

Deadman

Bill Sheldon's *Deadman* is like nothing you've ever read before, yet it speaks to the universal quandaries and possibilities present in wandering the mazes of our lives where "Purpose is assured only in the ground." *Deadman* shows us, through Sheldon's succinct and brilliant language, where and who we are and might be while reminding us to "Enjoy / the river rolling on your right, / the sunshine under a sky / so large it seems a question."

> —Caryn Mirriam-Goldberg, Poet Laureate of Kansas 2009-13, *How Time Moves: New and Selected Poems*

Deadman is the mythos of our times, a comedy of errors, a hodgepodge of Shakepeare, Fitzgerald, Eliot, and other dead guys; and he's living in a contradiction as he "has had enough of being / the one true deadman walking."

> —Dennis Etzel, Jr., *Everything Is Ephemera*

Retrieving Old Bones

The voice of this book is of this place in the best sense.

> —Steven Hind, *The Loose Change of Wonder*

When I Go West:
New and Selected Poems

Also by William Sheldon

Deadman (Spartan Press, 2021)

Rain Comes Riding (Mammoth Publications, 2011)

Into Distant Grass (Oil Hill Press, 2009)

Retrieving Old Bones (Woodley Press, 2002)

When I Go West:
New and Selected Poems

William Sheldon

MEADOWLARK PRESS

established 2014

EMPORIA, KANSAS

Meadowlark Poetry Press, LLC
meadowlarkbookstore.com
P.O. Box 333, Emporia, KS 66801

When I Go West: New & Selected Poems
Copyright © William Sheldon, 2025

Resale and Bulk Orders: For details, contact the publisher at info@meadowlark-books.com.
https://www.meadowlarkbookstore.com/resale-and-bulk-orders

Cover Photo: Scott Brown
Cover Design: TMS, Meadowlark Press
Interior Design: Linzi Garcia, Meadowlark Press
Author Photo: William Sheldon

POETRY / American / General
POETRY / Subjects & Themes / Nature
POETRY / Subjects & Themes / Family

Library of Congress Control Number: 2025944665

ISBN: 978-1-956578-83-6 (paperback)

For Cindy,

forever.

Contents

When I Go West

House Rules   3

What We Write About   4

After All   5

Time   6

Matins   7

Small Bill of Rights   8

Birdseed   9

With the Low Poppy Mallow   10

Our Son Is Leaving   11

Through Difficulty   12

Open Window   13

Smoke in the Distance   14

This World, Not the Next   15

The Strange Promise of Fall   16

Yes, I Said Perfect   17

Ad Astra Per Aspera   18

Our Present Sky   19

Body House Land Sky   21

Lying on the Lawn   22

Ungrassed, the Land   23

Caught   25

Helping the Needy   26

Low   27

The World and Oysters   28

Three Rivers   29

Benediction   31

Funereal   32

Right Now: Arkansas River   33

Hunting Arrowheads on the Arkansas 34
River Sartoris 35
Palimpsest 37
Thrall 38
I'd Like to Be There 39
A Better Heaven 40
What I Know Today 41
When I Go West 42

Retrieving Old Bones

Walking a Dirt Road 45
A Kind of Seeing 46
In Serious Cold 47
Western Kansas Boys 48
Road Hunting 49
Learning to Swim 50
First on the Scene 51
My Father Tells Me Bedtime Stories: Montana, 1966 52
Dear John 54
Trickster Over the Wire 55
Rafting the Martha Brae 56
At Our Dancing Away 57
Twins 58
Peter Pan Park: Emporia, Kansas 59
Retrieving Old Bones 60
The Last Mallard 62
Portents 63
Beside the Garage 64
Coyote Slips Through 66
One A.M. 68

After the Zoo 69

Fecund July 70

Kate, Who Is Just 72

Catching My Breath 73

Into Distant Grass

Two Days Before Spring 77

The Garden Done 78

Boards 79

My Neighbor's Fence 80

Murder, Suicide 82

Trimming the Tree 83

Winter at Forty-Two 84

The Pilings 85

Poem for Spring 87

Into Distant Grass 88

Attention 89

Water 90

The Perfect Poem 91

Sighting 92

Rain Comes Riding

Between the Fall Grass 95

Broken Knife at Forty-Five 96

Lightning Strike 97

Idyll 98

Rain Comes Riding 99

Driving the Heart 100

Three Views of the Deity   102
On an Island in the Keys   103
A Little Death   105
Spring And   108
Under Kansas   110
Prayer   111
One Day in Kansas   112
Wichita: A Star Rises   113
I-70 West   114
Things That Are True in Our Town   115
What We Know   116
Hearing the River   117
Sonnet 1.618   118
Seeing You Tonight, I Realized   119
Satori   120
Thin Ice   121

Deadman

1.   125
2.   126
3.   127
4.   128
29.   129
30.   130
31.   132
34.   133
35.   134

About the Author   135
Acknowledgments   137

When I Go West

House Rules

The world says hello and makes its promise,
its only one, and we are forced to live
with one eye on the hand we've shaken,
amid the beauty of trying to deny the bargain.
We wake each day to the mockingbird's
free verse before the sky goes blue
through eastern windows. Who knows
its next note? We drink black coffee
in the cool breeze, pull the blankets,
our robes, a little tighter, plant roses
in the sandy soil, move the lilies,
read a book after lunch. All end
on the last page. The afternoon warm
and full on our backs, sweat in our eyes,
we dream of evening's cold beer
while checking the tomatoes. All night,
stars spin over the house, headlights
sometimes lighting our walls, dreams
thrown in as part of the bargain.

What We Write About

After Harry Crews

Love is an eye socket
in a dry skull, a polled horn,
a closed suture, bone to bone.
The river, the sun, the wind
desiccate you or petrify you,
tumble you, move you on.

Love is a smell,
the one that remains
in skulls in the rain,
the dark recesses
between eating
and breathing.
There is only love
and its absence.

After All

You may spend your days
never loving someone
or your days with someone
never loving you. (Time
is too short for lies.)
One thing we know: we die.
You may tell yourself
there's more.
I'll not stop you.
But say you find the hole
in that theory you could drive
a god through, what then? How
do you proceed?
"Are we good," you want to know,
"or bad?" knowing the answer is
"Yes" and "turnips."
Where should you go from here?

Chickens walk the garden
that needs turning, and our sun
rides high. Across the road,
the ancient horse makes his stilted
way to grain, an older mule behind,
and early morning light on the grass
seems a metaphor of contentment,
not peace. There is the bitterness
of coffee in the cold air, and a cardinal
calling a would-be mate
in the Douglas fir behind me,
leading me to think maybe
I might love you after all.

Time

A cardinal calls, desperate lust
masquerading as bravado, counter-
point to the beeping machinery
in reverse. The coffee
goes cold. The dog lies
across the screen porch doorway
oblivious to the robin
pogoing two feet from her nose.
The day is waiting. The boats
are turned belly up. Tomatoes
green on the vine. Tomorrow's
not worth discussion.
You, with your book in your hand,
it is time for your la-la-la's,
your mi-mi-mi's. A flash
of red followed by a darker,
similar shape makes its way
into the greening trees.

Matins

Barefoot, I follow the dog
onto November's yellow grass
into a morning not rainy but wet.
We sniff the breeze, wait for any
birdcall to bleed into damp air.
Silence, even wind deadened
by mist. Light to our east,
day deciding what to be. Someone's
smoke far from our road scents
the lightest breeze, distant
highway's rush numbed
by cotton air. Feet growing cold,
it would be easy to turn,
go in, but here silhouettes of goats
graze the field across the road,
and smoke carries the memory of dreams.
Two geese, black against gray,
not calling, only whistle of wings.
Enough to make me stay,
waiting, some shoeless greedy monk,
for morning's next note.

Small Bill of Rights

A man should be able to sit—
having come from building tomato cages—
in the shade of maple trees watching pullets
follow the Rhode Island hen under the pear
tree, where sunflower and millet seed
has fallen from the feeder, should
be able to drink black coffee while a red hen
stares hard-eyed in hopes of a treat,
should be able to savor the whicker
of the roan mare he cannot see
but knows walks behind the hill
where the Bluestem waves
in the lightest wind which is just enough
to drive biting flies from his naked ankles,
as the air warms, as he steels himself
to deal with the burrs growing in the bare
patch along the fence
where the chickens dust and a blue jay
sails free into the field beyond.

Birdseed

The ladder-backed woodpecker
hangs from the underside
of the suet cage. Eleven
new chicks scratch the grass
in their pen as their mother
has shown them. Four
house finches, scarlet
heads flashing
in morning light, take short
shifts in the birdbath.
Three new bluebirds
follow their parents
into the mown field
beside our house.
The song sparrow chicks
in the nest in the rain
gutter cry "Hungry"
when their father nears,
grub in his beak.
The one red-winged
blackbird that visits our yard
rests on the feeder. And then
amid all this
bounty, the epiphany
we have sought all summer,
there, at the sugar water,
the first hummingbird.

With the Low Poppy Mallow

The field is redolent with spiderwort;
a rich breeze chatters the cottonwood.
Clouds pass telling the story of rain
but don't stay for us to hear the end.
The dog whines wanting breakfast,
as the coffee goes cold. I would rather
not move, taking this in. I am here
with the low poppy mallow, the yarrow,
and the house finch on the edge
of the rain gutter, his red head a signal,
as sycamore and cottonwood seeds
blow from the roof. When the bluestem
moves in waves on the small hill
across the road, it scalds my heart
like hard rain.

Our Son Is Leaving

The dirt roads we've run
or walked at evening
are paved under. No dust
rises from them now.
No dog walks with me.
His ashes feed our garden,
and they have moved the highway
closer to our home. Nights,
our windows open, I
hear folks going, passing through.
Mornings, the mockingbird
in the maple behind our house
runs his nine-song repertoire,
each note his own; each
belongs to someone else. I pass
old man Moran, retreating
to his house, mail in his hand.
His wife, who gardened against
our fence, scolding our barking
Lab, has followed the dog
on his long route. A turkey calls
from the hillside, a young tom.
He fans his feathers
for the hen hopping on her
one good foot, their eyes
on my approach. She flattens
into grass, nearly disappearing.
As I pass, his brave display
wavers, then flares full,
a marvel in evening's sun.

Through Difficulty

In the raking light of a western sun,
the flowering crab—a Thunderchild—sits
just outside the shadow of the Bradford pear,
which lost a third of itself to the ice
that turned out our lights for six days.
We cooked soup on the wood stove,
read by candles, showered at the Y.
Logs from that tree rise from that stove,
on days the weather dips. But now is July.
102 the bank's sign claims.
Our Labrador, young and froggy,
drags a maple limb fallen
from the neighbor's tree into our yard.
Her predecessor's ashes mix in our garden
where tomatoes fail to redden.
Flies hang on the screen, signaling
a storm. The hen, with the foot hurt
by hail, crow-hops to the water font.
The sun drops below the line of cottonwoods
two fields over. A fingernail moon
rises cradling the first star. Kansans all,
we make our narrow way.

Open Window

The dog, who will bark when wind changes hands,
sleeps through traffic on the new highway
a quarter mile closer than its ancestor,
barely stirs at the foot of the bed when the train's horn
turns my sleep to dreams of distance and longing.
                                                    If I wake,
my thoughts become a headlamp
shining along the rails, searching out
the old Plymouth stalled on the tracks, calculating
time and space needed to stop
all that speeding steel behind me.
                                        Or perhaps
the dog wakes me, her kicking feet
or low whimper from her own dark dreams,
as a semi gears down near the city limits.
A great horned owl calls
from the Bradford pear in the back yard.
                                              The Plymouth's
engine catches, ancient blue fins rocket forward
off the tracks seconds before I pass.
                                        Breeze
shifts, blows against the traffic sounds,
the dog's breathing now low snoring.
                                        A thought
of someone kind to me at just the moment of need.
                                              The train
moves on down the tracks into moonless
night under the stars' dead light.

Smoke in the Distance

We stoke the wood stove at the patio's
edge, pull our chairs a little closer,
tug the Mexican blankets a little tighter.
The cold, dark beer is bitter.
We like the bite, the way
one does in later days, sensation
welcomed.
      Smoke
rises from the near horizon confirming
life in the distance, night
and winter coming on.

This World, Not the Next

Circled by his yard light, my neighbor,
surprised again by his ninetieth year,
closes the door of the red barn
across the field and the north-south road
west of our house, hitches himself
up into his red truck and drives away.
What stays is the black fringe of leafless trees
against the horizon, pierced by another
yard light a mile behind, and the red lights
of the radio tower farther still, that
and the pink-orange of evening
that follows us everywhere.
The wrought iron chair is cold against my back
sitting here at the garden's verge, a colder
bourbon in my hand. Mid-fall
and my elbow still aches from summer's
hammering—the stone wall that must
come down, the new roof, the chickens'
coop and pen—aches each time the glass
rises, as my knee hollers each time
I stand. I am sure I have felt better
than this moment. Perhaps
I will never feel this good again. Still,
I will say it now: except to fix
a fence or to weed the beans, I'll not
knock wood or kneel. Our universe spins on,
its own equation, a comfort against
this growing cold and the last light
of a sky I love each time I see it, no matter
its form. Tonight, when I lie down, what follows
is sleep, just sleep, whether I wake or no.

The Strange Promise of Fall

There is icy beer and a cold metal chair
under the orange-pink sky
with winter coming on. We talk across the glass-
topped table, staring into the field beyond the fence
where once our neighbor mowed all summer
around a killdeer nest, always one parent
playing the hurt wing, distracting the growling
green beast, easy prey if the thing would just
stray from the clutch of eggs, the chicks.
That same neighbor fed cat food to the fox
and her kits who denned first under our culvert
and then his barn until they, like the killdeer,
disappeared. "Every year," he told me, "when I cut hay,
a fox shows up following my tractor, hunting mice.
He makes sure I see him, then falls in behind me."
My neighbor, ninety-three this year, himself
has disappeared. I see his daughter's car in the drive,
imagine her wondering which pictures, awards,
books to keep, what any of it means. No basement,
we have a shed full of ornaments, books we've no
shelves for, despite our many shelves, toys of youth,
bows I no longer shoot. Our children would be
best served, when that time comes, to build a fire
for us, the house, the shed, watching smoke rise
in the brisk sky, tasting cold, dark, beer, the kind
December demands. Glad I am, I'll not be there,
but sad too not to finger one more time a flint
arrowhead found on a gravel bar as I stepped from my canoe,
not to read again the underlined passage of a dog-eared
page, to feel again the strange promise of fall,
the way spring was once, and then summer. I could stay
here in this chair, in this darkening light, if one would refill
my glass, but the young Labrador has arrived, rubber ball
in her mouth, and you have moved inside to check the dinner
we threw together, and the glass won't fill itself.
I have made my peace with fall. Let winter come as it will.

Yes, I Said Perfect

The young Labrador whines
at the back door a half acre
from my chair in the corner
of the yard. A small breeze
moves through bluestem,
brown now on the hillside
across the road. Chickens
dust in the garden, empty
but for marigolds
and bermuda, where tomatoes,
beans, and okra reigned
over summer's hours.
In horsetail clouds
above our house, a sundog's
suddenness takes my breath.
I think, as I do daily, even
under light less perfect
over cottonwoods
going yellow, something
the puppy, the pullets take in
like air. Simple as dirt, it breaks me
every time I say it:
"I love this world." And now,
at least, never want to leave.

Ad Astra Per Aspera

The dog's ashes sift a little lower
in the garden under evening's arterial light.
Above, Venus calls in the west,
and the last flight of geese settles
in old man Moran's pond.
Hunched and shuffling, he makes his way
to feed the old horse and graying mule,
a fortnight from the end of his wife's
long fight. Stars are winking now, but
we've difficulty enough below.

Our Present Sky

i. Under Kansas Stars

A thin smile at our foolishness,
the moon turns from us with vain hope
for our improvement upon her return.
West we pull precious water
for corn only our cars will drink.
Ours is a drought of imagination,
desiring oil at a spigot's twist.
We bless Wyoming coal cars passing
at the crossing. East, our leaders,
children at recess, make mischief,
pull legs off spiders, wings
off flies, burn ants because they can.
Under the sliver of the first quarter moon,
the lesser prairie-chicken does the ghost dance.

ii. Over Our Town

These birds circling above, black
wings fingering the lightest updraft,
may hold no interest in us,
for now, but they smell carrion
for miles. They wheel over our town,
the hands of nature's clock. Not abstract
time, they are emissaries from reality
beyond philosophy or religion's
Rube Goldberg mousetraps of imagination.
Their beaks and featherless heads
brook no attempt to turn them cute,
remind us of business at hand and time
left to do it. They grow in number,
almost a hundred, a spectacle.
We avert our gaze under hard bird eyes.

iii. Our Present Sky

Long-armed, cold-fingered, the stars
reach to us from a past we
barely imagine in our steepest
dreaming. Their message is simplest,
perhaps the only: This comes
to us all. Mostly, we
choose to not listen, gussying
up their light, making baubles
of their beauty: skulls polished
by sand in the wash of sudden flood.
We see the dead behind us as a mire
of missteps as we fumble, fearful,
through a forest we have yet to reach.
Meanwhile, the sun is going down,
or coming up in its great splendor.
Our present sky is waiting.

Body House Land Sky

Your breath
rising, passing
through the gates of your teeth
weds with our air becoming this
poem.

This house
will fall, a fate
desirous, if not sought,
coffin cutters turning its ribs
to dirt.

River
falling downhill
carves curves through patient land
watching as water winds its way
to sea.

Above
this house, our talk
echoed by the river's blab,
in ceaseless tension, waits an end-
less sky.

Lying on the Lawn

If you lower your head far enough,
you can hear—below the soughing
of ethereal breeze in the fescue
and the professional chat of ants—
the dirt's whisper: "Choose
your position well," it murmurs.
"Make it one you can live with
forever." If you wait, I swear
you'll hear the low laughter
of a hundred friends.

Ungrassed, the Land

i. Natures

In the best world, we are all
who we should be, following
a nature we cannot resist. This,
then, is the best world. True
to our nature, we can look
about us, see what we have done.
We, though, think we can change
ourselves, our nature. Here
on our high perch, let us look
again. Let us contemplate
what we do next.

ii. The Cell

We walk a graveyard daily,
earth the accretion of all
that has come.
We should fear it less,
and death. We should go
upon our way with respect.
It is a cell that cannot
divide, one we will not
escape. When birds
begin to foul their nests,
their mothers force them out.
Ours is forbearing, but her eye
is hard as any bird's, and you
cannot fly.

iii. The Dust

West of here waits the dust on the wind's
next convoy. Ungrassed, the land
gives itself up to the breath of each passing breeze.
Voracious and careless in our usage,
what comes to pass, we have wrought,
though we take all but the blame.
It is an old story: In the dust
that coats the tables of those
houses without conditioned air lies the history
of all our foolishness and the bad luck
of running out of time. It is not
just wind the dust awaits. The passing
of massive time is something like hope.

Caught

It is common in low water
to find their marks on every
gravel bar, so the walker
was not surprised
to see one there, rapt
in secret ecstasy,
wrist twisting the throttle
as his four wheels
cut a deepening circle,
roar of gravel and water
spewing behind him.

And when the rider stopped,
raised his goggles to see
this thing he'd made,
it was as a toddler
newly trained, fascinated
with what he'd left
behind, but when he saw
the walker there
staring, perhaps troubled,
certainly bemused,
it was as a pubescent boy,
his mother blundering through
a door he thought locked.

But the walker was not
his mother and felt no need
to reassure him that it was
only natural, but instead
stood, a kind of badge,
as the rider pulled down
his goggles and rode upriver.

Helping the Needy

Between his bones and clothes he barely wears
there is the thinnest kind of intercourse.
Those clothes, woven more of the scent of piss
and sweat than of thread, have made him easy
pickings for charity's badge and truncheon,
offering up a lesson with its cot.
He has come to patient understanding
of those who would make salvation the price
of food, who would rack him on the altar
of good deeds. He takes their money, smiles, nods,
in ways to ease their consciences. They leave
believing they have done some good. He walks
away—leaving their silver with busking
musicians who thank him—without a word.

Low

She lives somewhere between fret strike
and the guitar's whisper, her skin
like feathers moving or the stoicism
of oaks. In the yard are chickens,
skinks, switchgrass, and the growl of smoke
and water. In here, only ink black
coffee, blood oranges, and the clay drip
of time. She feels her blood twist, longing
for more than the murmur of cotton.
She would scent manure and silage, gaze
upon dappled crabgrass under apple trees.
She would dodge, if she could,
the wool hammer of her days. She saw a painting
once, medieval villagers dancing
to bagpipes and drinking beer
from booming steins, none of them
smiling. She sets aside the barely-plucked
guitar, stares long at the blind-drawn window.

The World and Oysters

He brought rakia and she brought flowers.
The food was good. They left with colds.

He brought flowers. The rakia was good.
He left without eating, walking home in the cold.

The food was cold. There were flowers.
She was cold. There was rakia.

He brought food for her cold.
They drank rakia. Bees moved in the flowers.

He drank warm rakia with honey
for his cold, called her flower when she brought food.

He went without food to buy her rakia.
She was a frozen flower with bee-stung lips.

Three Rivers

i. Night Noise

Smoke rises in horns
on a heron's wind.
All night the mud groans
as the river sweats.
We hear the moon
scratching its cradle.
Stepping from our tent
onto this pelt of sand,
all is still
except the slight
panting of smoke.

ii. Commonplaces at a Wake

The rain's mourning
holds the river enthralled:
the drizzle's starched talk
with the soughing mud:
"Tomorrow . . . A better day . . .
No, no . . . A long way from
happiness, but . . . The sun
will rise . . . Some compassionate
gesture . . . " The river
who barely knew the departed
watches the mud,
knows that surface
acceptance of solid advice
belies the cold scream
that is building.

iii. Coldwater

West of our town, the bones
of the river lie whitening.
Nights we hear mud weep
regretting a lover's leaving,
perhaps even the loving,
as the distracted moon
hums above. We
know the river's secrets
are ours. We smile
through soiled lips,
our streets coils of skin,
the bones of our hearts
cradling thorns awaiting
evening's exhaust and desire.
Singing down the sun,
we make our sad ways
to that trickle of solace
knowing what we have done
we will again.

Benediction

In Blackriver, the last church
boarded its doors four years ago.
The other two are a boarding house
and a donut shop, The Holey Cruller,
where they hold service each time
someone dies. No one says "passes."
Folks gather for donuts
and coffee so black its depth
seems endless. If she
was ninety-eight and died asleep,
they talk through smiles,
and only the neighbor
who checked in on her, realizing
one duty less, tears up when she
returns the key she used
when the dead woman's son
traveled out of town. Talk
of who ran the tractor
into the granary, of the blind
uncle who killed the young hog
with one stroke of his stock cane,
runs into the waning light.
Friends file out, leaving
a shrinking knot of family.
An ex-elder stands post
at the door, shaking hands.
Those leaving, still tasting
the sweetness of unraised donuts
and the bitterness of strong coffee
hear him whisper,
"This world, not the next."

Funereal

We donned our death hair,
read the rain maps,
and hied on a hawk's wind
down to Deep River,
with its mud musk and dust
broth, its sad smothered
sun under clouds, parting
for a fingernail moon
to scratch the hair-ash
streets, and starlit water
snakes whipsawing the current
where the mud-toothed river
chewed the town's brink.

Death herons rose
cacophonous, chorale-throated
in the creosote wind
whining through salt cedar
while grass marched
on pampas legs
toward destiny undreamt,
the end of the engine-
throated river.

Preordained under moon-throb
we dragged the drossy body
to the mossy font
dressed in daily togs,
fingernails dirty and unpared:
spare words in the silt rot,
dipped and dropped
in a reedy canoe, taken
into the river-grip,
the grass-walk, downstream.
"These are the days,"
we say, burning our hair
in Deep River's streets.

Right Now: Arkansas River

The current moves as fast as its volume,
gravity, and the banks' resistance allow.
It is good to look ahead,
where the river shallows on a bar,
where a deadfall makes passage
a prickly thing.
         It is also good to note
the red of the cardinal in the cottonwood's heart-
shaped leaves, calling for a mate and the hammering
of a woodpecker deeper in the trees,
and the light on the gravel polished, right
now, by the water moving your canoe.

Hunting Arrowheads on the Arkansas

Eleven egrets rose
over the river bend, over green shrubs
even a droughty river holds
as had another flock two days ago
right before he saw the small Washita,
a white triangle in the pea gravel—
he might have, had he believed
in omens, egret deities, or other magic,
thought himself lucky, looked
for another point, that moment,
at his feet. Instead, he was only
gladdened by rising birds. All day he saw
gravel and minnows, light
on the water. Only later,
moving back upriver,
did he indulge his foolishness,
cursing, almost aloud, the day's
heat, the barrenness of the river.
He saw again the ungainly grace
of wading egrets lifting in late
afternoon's sallow light. Their blessing
had been real. "Walk slowly, look hard
in the small gravel. Move on."

River Sartoris

Sometimes a knife won't take an edge
becoming only a weight
you choose to carry, or leave behind,
despite the day you found it close
beside the arrowhead, small
stemmed heart, sparkling among gravel,
as you waded from the river onto the bar.
The finely worked flint hangs
in a frame, but the little knife, once
you knocked off the rust and whet it,
has stayed in your pocket for years, called on
to sever twine, never cut the first time,
or dig a thorn, but it would not stay sharp.
So, the day comes when you're cutting rope,
sawing really, and are forced
to walk back to the shed for a better blade.
It is an old idea—of religion, say, or governance,
the workings of the world—you've held
dear and true so long it's like your heart
working quietly, laboring till it goes bad.
You hold it against your palm, weighing
your thoughts, saying good-bye
before you set it on the shelf, drop it
in a drawer, but do not give it to your son,
knowing how jaggedly
a dull blade cuts. That arrowhead hangs
framed on the wall, five hundred years
old, exquisitely chipped, sharp
despite the river's tumbling,
never to be hafted again.
Step from the gravel, back
into the heart of a new current.

ii.

Sometimes it happens at evening,
when, without the three-quarter moonlight,
wading upstream would seem foolish,
ankles caught by logs along the shoreline,
stumbling into chest-deep holes.
As you crawl along a deadfall
in such feeble light, you marvel
at peace passing your understanding.
As you make your way
down off this pile of limbs into pampas
grass and salt cedar, what little light
is left seems perfect. Coyotes singing
close in a field above the bank
match the pitch and yaw of Earth's turning.
All this strikes you like a stick snapping
back into place. The river is a koan
perhaps rather than a poem. You wade on,
knowing it will be dark
before you reach your truck at the bridge,
pleased by this discovery.

iii.

Wading cold water upriver,
under the skirl of paired hawks hunting,
you find a dog's jawbone skimming pea gravel,
smooth and clean in your hand.
Dropped,
   it moves again
a different direction from yours,
the same destination.

Palimpsest

Swallows circle from the bridge,
cursive against the sky, their shadows
gestures on this leaf of the river.
Underneath the lives of wind
and current—glyphs
of minnows' short passage
through the shallows,
broad strokes of carp
against the current, a truck
on the bridge, the stuttering
cry of a Kingfisher who dips
and drips interlocking rings—
patterns merge, fading in evening
light until the layers are lost,
all ink the same ink.
It is only days later,
when the Eastern Kingbird
hovering above Bluestem,
quills in the breeze,
snatches a rising moth, that I
begin to discern the first word.

Thrall

I like to walk the river far
from the bridge into the sound
of no traffic
hearing a kingfisher dive
or water snake slide
in S's on the surface
I like to see no colorful
kayaks, or canoes, pass me
wading crotch-deep into holes
where carp hold   their fins
feathering the current
knowing no one anywhere
walks like I do
subject of all I survey

I'd Like to Be There

at the last of people
some evening when the sky
looks like now
through this airport window
trees still green reaching
into rich clouds unaware
of our passing
to sit behind this glass
in a concourse bereft
of passengers
watching late afternoon sun
waiting for some flock
to find this square of blue
I want to rise and walk out
the front door that still
slides open into the day's
heavy humidity
into coming night finding
my way to the interstate
in unrequited love
with the quiet
last man on the road
both crumbling
and happy to

A Better Heaven

Sun and wind
wind on the water
leaves in the current
things a river tumbles
bleached white crawfish
shell of its former self
flake of flint worked
into a knife
cutting only current
coyote femur   heron feather
and someday perhaps me
or you if time
catches you
Upstream you tumble
breathless on some gravel bar
begin your slow exchange
with the world
Maybe those who'd
look for you are gone
so no one finds you
High water dislodges
some part of you
tibia say or ulna
to return the way you came
A canoeist more interested
in seducing a rowing mate
than lessons lifts you
holds you up to the sunlight
drops you in the shallows
to wait
for high water

What I Know Today

The opposite of life is . . .
Well, death's opposite is hunger.
"Love and death," the poet
says, "love and death." Horsetail
clouds framed by a window tease
dying leaves, red in setting sun.
  Bah.
All preamble to my saying again
how much I love this graveyard
we tread daily. Let me walk thigh-
deep in the river, sit under winter's
red skies. We can be friends, but dirt
is my only lover. We will lie together,
rise in each other's clothes.

When I Go West

It will be paddling upriver
past floating leaves.
There will be no need
to ice the beer.
I'll find the right place,
or my arms will tire.
Some gravel bar or island
in the current
will suffice, large enough
for one last walk,
turning stones, picking
out a bison tooth,
a piece of ossified bone.
I'll eat the sardines
I've brought, drink the beer,
stretch out in winter's
welcome sand
to wait for spring.

Retrieving Old Bones

Walking a Dirt Road

I kick up a rock,
ask my son, who is six,
What's this look like?
Arrow, he says. I
was thinking heart.
                         Suddenly,
the whispered trill of quail
from the brush
at our right. We turn
watch them make their short way
into grass
behind the fence.
                       There was
a time when, gun or not,
my hands came up
right eye sighting
a point where a bird was
about to be.
                   Now,
my hands stay
but a place
in my heart's beating
tries to remember—pick
a single bird. Remembers
the confusion of the covey's pattern
and the patterns
of shot touching nothing.
And a boy's anger.
                       What are they?
Tyler asks.
I breathe once, choosing carefully
my first word.

A Kind of Seeing

Uncle Walt walked
the old Crook place
blinder than a rock,
swinging his stock cane
with spiteful accuracy
on the old cow
when she crowded
my lugging of the grain.
Or halted me with it
at the waist
   "Watch that wire"
before I felt its metal bite.

Once he hooked me
ass-end over appetite
from a half stack of bales,
and before my wind was back,
lifted coils
gently from the straw
and slid the diamondback
off into the whispering grass.
And to my "Kill it,"
his dusty voice,
"There's worse than snakes."

In Serious Cold

I struggled under the box
full of Ry's freezing
dead Weimaraner.
Eighty goddamned pounds
of "a good dog"
in a shipping crate, moving toward
a row of trees on the horizon
I hoped he remembered,
to bury in a hole
too large to dig by nightfall,
in dirt too hard to turn
that mean-mouthed sonofabitch
that bit the head from
every bird I ever
shot behind him. Ryan
blubbering,
wheezing toward the spot,
and probably a coronary.
Me knowing that if I had
to carry his dying ass
out of that dry river bed
I'd have to bow
out, and that crate
not big enough for them both.
My nerves belting out,
"Let it go. Let it go."
as duty drove us on.

Western Kansas Boys

We walked our quail poor
fields, teeth set. "Remember
that covey last year." No dog
and four shot, expecting
the night train rumblings
of pheasant, not
the soft explosion at our cuffs
we desired. Surprised once,
no meadowlark lifting from
the corners of our hard eyes
was wholly safe.

Road Hunting

We spotted dark
oriental
heads in tall grass
sighting
pheasants at forty
sometimes fifty
miles an hour
  all the clichés
hitting the brakes
bailing out
barrels everywhere
snapshooting sprinting
into the ditch
past the posted sign
a hand full of feathers
back on the road
Americans

Learning to Swim

What I remember most
of the one time
I saw my father drunk
was the awful grace
of his falling
silently
under the "Flying Dutchman"
through a sea of folding chairs
plunging
grabbing one chair-
back then another
to have each in succession
crawl away,
staying somehow,
between momentum and resistance,
almost afloat,
lips tight eyes wide until
miraculously
he broke free,
breast against the bar.
And my strange pride
in the beauty of it.

First on the Scene

It wasn't the imagined
concussion that held
the cub reporter,
camera to his eye,
but what would have followed
the hubcap's drunken roll
and soft clatter on the shoulder
half in the grass.
He tried to hear the silence, the world
catching its breath—

    the head on the seatback
    beneath the spidered glass, mouth
    open as if asleep—

before the newly made dew
woke with birds.

My Father Tells Me Bedtime Stories: Montana, 1966

i. Speed Graphic

When Patterson and his deputy
pulled them out of the old Merc'
sawed in half on that phone pole . . .
I knew no one could have . . .
When she groaned,
Pat almost dropped her.

They sprawled her dead boyfriend
out in the broken glass
not a scratch on him, just
a piss stain getting bigger.
And her . . .
windshield gravel in her cheek,
blood turning her clothes black,
screaming, as her brain woke up.

I popped a few flashes
before I puked.

ii. Grizzly

Summer-ranger told me
the two who were left half-fell
from that damn jack pine
like bad fruit.
Said he watched
them pick through damp cloth.

One boy said they'd left
the trail.
Woke that night
to his snuffling.
Fought out of their bags
and climbed.

The other boy said he'd pressed
his face bloody against the bark
trying not to hear her . . .

"It's eating me!"

He kept saying how happy
he'd been when that stopped.

iii. Jack Pine Savage

The boys at Nash's told me
that eventually the city kid
might not have felt
what those corks
were doing to his face.
"The wrong words
to the wrong man," one said.
Nash said, "After a time, he quit
trying to turn away."
But they could still hear him groan
as the spikes came down
before Nash
stepped from behind the bar
to stop it.

Dear John

Crouched in damp cattails,
I did not see the dove
blasting
from the spiral of blackbirds
until it was too late
to raise the gun.

That afternoon,
the note
fell back to the table.
The other birds
   their soft vacant eyes
went to hell
in the bed of the truck.

Trickster Over the Wire

He had known her
for miles on the wind
before his nose
was at her throat.

The fence meant next to nothing.

She smelt the faint
blood at his muzzle
and the wild god in his fur.
Watched him shimmer
just outside the yard light's
grasp
before becoming again
a hole
in the dark.

Rafting the Martha Brae

David, the Rasta-man,
shows us black-tipped white
wings of jackal egrets,
all spice, sugarcane, fresh
water shrimp. Laughs

in back of the raft
with my wife
while I pole, half-assed,
down the river.

We are overtaken
by silver-haired brass,
their raftsman's face
a knot, eyes
of Texas upon him.
One ol' gal twangs, "How long
will we be out here?"
"Soon come," he says.
"Not long."
David smiles,
all but his eyes.
Says to no one,
"Not long enough
to know."

At Our Dancing Away

How far away can we go
before we return through the back door
to this room where friends,
thinking we are still gone, talk
about us, not recognizing
me in my new beard, or you in Gypsy clothes?
What are they saying? "Just
like them to . . . " You smile, nudging
my ribs. We fill our pockets
with food we have paid for and my hat
with wine, and just when
                                they almost
see me in the dour face on the mantle, just
as they are rubbing their eyes to look
again, we will slide out the front, bumping
into yet another guest who will turn
long enough to scratch his head
at our dancing away. He is the one
who will find the note: "There is Tupperware
in the pantry, foil in the second drawer.
Any half-full bottles are yours. Put out
the cat. He can find his way."

Twins

Holding him at the mirror,
I watch my son,
his brother lost at birth,
reach this first time
for his own hand.

Peter Pan Park: Emporia, Kansas

Six months from the day
we received your ashes,
the day we carried to your brother,
in his isolette, that first
small sack of your mother's milk,
we have come to this little stage
of sod and stone.

To this place where youth
is held, where the day
Grandfather died,
friends and I tumbled
in burlap bags
on my seventh birthday, past
the memorial to the dead girl,
past the swings, to this place
where your brother cries,
reaching in hunger from his blanket,
where your mother and I first
took up hands,
where we now . . .
            We cannot
make the words.
We let the wind take you,
left
to find our way
to the car,
and to your brother's feeding,
uncertain of our hands.

Retrieving Old Bones

The lightning drives him
upstairs
where his bad teeth
deny my dreams.
I wake to his black bulk wedged
beneath the bed frame
to drag him down
sixteen stairs,
each an agony
for his crippled hips.

Two weeks later,
gone for days,
the pound will call.
"Over the fence," they'll say.
A Springer bitch. Her
owner hot. And again,
it will cost me
more than his price
to drag him home.

Almost drowned him once
on a winged mallard
out deep enough I
nearly filled my waders
dragging him in to wait
for the drake to sicken
and drift to shore.

"He always ranged a bit,"
my neighbor says,
sighting him once
on the shoulder

of the bypass
dragging a chunk of limestone,
and once head high
with an antler
retrieved
fresh from some garage.

So we are not surprised,
after a week of dragging
himself to water,
to find him gone. But the pound
doesn't hold him. And no
body. My father tells me
he's heard a Lab
will find a pond
and hold himself
under
as long as it takes.

The Last Mallard

Closing my eyes that night
I saw the pairs
and small V's
track across gray sky
until sleep.

In the blind had come a point
when green heads and orange feet
lay like things
too fine
for steel shot
and dog spit.

Sighting along the bluing
into gray, I halted
follow-through
                    and missed,
forever.

This spring, I see them
paired in ditch water—green
head going to blue, her
patterned browns—perfect
in evening's light.
                    Yesterday,
you flew lone across my road: Wildest
of all things, I
held your eye.

Portents

Newly moved to the edge of town,
I awoke to signs—
red-tailed dragging a bull snake
up air, apparition of
                    a fawn
from grass too short to hold him—
careful lest I miss some omen—
elm filled with the white fruit
of egrets, snake skin
under the chokecherry
at the garden's edge. You know,
the big things.
                    I was slow to notice
chipping sparrows dusting
in the field beside the house—
their sudden choreographed
lift into trees
when swallows showed.
Slow to learn that all these
mean the same way.

Beside the Garage

i.

Such decadence in squirrels—
picking crab apples, biting
them once, and letting them
                        fall
again
and again, until the drive
is awash with pulp
and flies. I,
with my rake, am a heretic
among hedonists.

ii.

With each step into the mulch
of last fall's forgotten leaves
and this year's crab apples,
flies rise from their cloying treats.

I bring the rake.

"Sorry boys, your salad days
are over."

iii.

In the mulch I find one
dead cicada—slightly iridescent
still—one centipede, one albino
cricket. Dubious treasures all.

iv.

Twice I have moved the last
remnants of the leaf pile
from the woodlouse's path.
Again, he swerves into the leaves.

Little coffin-cutter, I think this
is a journey you
were meant to make.

v.

Awaiting Friday and the city's
harried bearers, three
lawn bags—strange chrysalides—slump
against the garage.
                    Imagine
their bursting over the land-
fill's compost heap,
new shapes winging
against a fervid sky,
before settling, leaves
to leavings and dust
to dust.

Coyote Slips Through

Coyote slips through
the fence of my dreams,
runs amok, inciting
the blue-blooded curs
of the neighborhood
to yip and howl.

I wake and walk
naked into the backyard.
From across the road
a sound like familiar
lovers in an old bed.
The neighbors'
cutting horse, scratching
her rump against the fence,
stops to look behind.
I follow her eyes, and there
you are,
little bastard wolf,
paused, dreaming yourself
big enough to make a meal
of old man Moran's mare.
But she knows
your lonesome ways
and returns to the rhythms
of the fence.
You drop your head,
move on, past
the Welsh Corgi the neighbors
have named Coyote.
I hear him yap once, imagine
his diving through the pet door,
lucky that you are sated
on mice and young rabbits.

I piss, wondering again
how far I could run
barefoot, and if I could find
covering by winter.
I head in
to where my wife
is sleeping, her legs
kicking lightly
in her dreams.

One A.M.

Having limped the Olds
home from Rip Griffin's
in Limon, Colorado,
where we walked
                for hours
in circles of heat
and grasshoppers
waiting
for the new water pump,
I lie down
        and
at the point of sleep,
watch a sidewinder curl
out in the sands
behind my eyes, hear
my dead uncle, "Don't step
behind that mule."
Then my father's voice,
emphatic—
        "Bill."
I sit up, listening
for breath—
my wife's
        my son's
                the dog's.
I decide to check the closets.

After the Zoo

The smell of the snake house
lingers
flavoring even the salsa
over beans and rice
I share with my son,
nearly three. Herpetarium,
where he ran glass
to glass,
shouting, "What is this?
What is this
thing?" Blessed boy,
holds up a grape and,
working a new
and favorite phrase,
asks, "Is it perfect?"
I smile. "Is it
good?"
"Yes," I say. "It is."

Fecund July

The moon lifts, full
as a muskmelon
above an evening pregnant
with the desperation of cicadas,
pulling waves of mosquitoes
from the ditch water. My hands
are speckled with my own
blood. Tomorrow
I will pull ticks, full
as lima beans, from the Labrador's
shoulders.
            But this morning
it was weeds and
rapacious Bermuda that would
rather grow in the garden
than the yard. I redirected
tendrils of watermelon
from the fence.
            In the distance
an estate sale, and the auctioneer's
"Who'll give me . . ." I imagined
his silver Stetson tilted
back on his head, a halo in mid-
morning sun, like
Bob Brown's.
            My sisters and I
three and five, picking a watermelon
from his patch, our parents'
full laughter with Bob and his pregnant
wife. "Those melons'll cross
with anything," nodding to her swelling
belly, and saying to me, too young
to get it, "I told her not to
come out here in no sundress."

                    Inside,
with perfect calm, waits my wife.
Three months left of bed rest. Our
doctor, remembering an earlier life
in vet school, says, "I'll be glad
to get this little one
on the ground."
                    I return
to the house bearing
offerings. Full tomatoes, their rain
split skin spilling seeds, staining
my shirtfront, and a melon
so ripe it will crack
at the knife's lightest touch.
Greedy, we will eat,
waiting for fall, laughing
at the juice on our cheeks,
tasting the damp heat of sun
and earth and rain.

Kate, Who Is Just

walking, moves through the hall
into the living room,
eyes closed, giggling,
as she careens
into a wall, or bumps
her head upon the sofa table. She
is the climber. She,
not her older brother,
will want the motorcycle.
Myself an older brother,
I am choosing wisely
my fairy tales: talismans
against wolves
and huntsmen. She
is choosing which chair
needs scaling, which
door tried, which cabinet emptied,
ascending too fast for my fretting.
I must content myself
with lifting her off
of the breakfast table,
the back of the couch,
where she dances,
smiling. I must learn
to trust that she sees
more of her own life,
even behind closed eyes,
than I, stare as I might.

Catching My Breath

A clear night and I hear Canada
geese talking their way
over our house. Everyone else
asleep, I lie
here on the couch
with these poems, making notes,
thinking how yesterday's
light touched spring geese pulling
late January sky. After weeks of snow,
my son and I driving home,
windows open,
"Mariachi Loco" on Mexican radio,
Tyler flailing, dancing loco in his seat,
laughing until I'm sure he'll pee,
closing a day sprawled
on the sofa, reading, not
teaching
                or grading. And then
the geese, in evening's perfect light.
And the mallards—her patterned browns
aglow, his head the green
of a world that creates
a moment where I can believe
all this will hold.
                        And against it all,
the clear laughter of a miracle
boy born three months early
as we return to a mother,
wife whose heart's blood
I saw on surgeon's shoes
just three quick years ago, and
so, I always knock wood, even
with none around. But because

there is, I'll knock, finish
these notes, and go
to Cindy where she sleeps
(and tonight, I'll say this)
fretfully without me.

Into Distant Grass

Two Days Before Spring

My daughter navigates freshly tilled earth
where we will plant potatoes. My son
throws a clod into the field beside our yard.
The lights below clouds bellying the horizon
fires the rust on the burn barrel, on my children's
red hair. One state west, their great-grandmother
is dying. Again, my daughter has me right
the canoe in the garden corner so she
can play inside. This evening
is a tease, says our weatherman. Tomorrow
it will snow. Doctors offer
nothing so definite. Last night
she seemed ready. Grandchildren called, hoping
she could hear. This morning, life
fought up again. My daughter lies still
in the hull of the canoe, eyes closed,
giggling when I rock it. It is cooling. Something
is on the move. My son finds a tomato stake,
laughs, staggers with it under his armpit, falls,
the sky ablaze behind the canoe, the fence.

The Garden Done

We pulled cilantro
gone too early to coriander
while a desperate cardinal sang out his red heart
in midsummer heat.
We fought our plot—potatoes,
dug too soon, beetles at their leaves,
lettuce souring in the heat, grasshoppers
on the tomatoes, caterpillars on the dill—
reaping a mild winter
and then fierce July. On our walks,
May's cardinals sang at every phone pole.
June we talked of how the garden never
looked so good. Then July. August,
I turned forty-one. In the paper,
oil company scientists said the globe
is not warming. We read vasectomies
sometimes spontaneously reconnect.
You were late that month
in sympathy. In such heat, hope
and fear are two verses of one song.

Boards

The way you can sand a joint
until the crack almost disappears,
the grain in two boards seeming
to meet in a sane pattern. So too
should be all my endeavors—
playing catch with my children,
weeding the garden, making love
with my wife, writing this poem.

But there is a restlessness in boards,
born of long stillness in the trunk,
while the slim, ethereal top branches
shimmered in the nomad breeze,
while the leaves yearly deserted,
and the roots sought new pools.
So when they can,
boards will warp
giving themselves
up to the will of water, moving
in what little ways they can.

My Neighbor's Fence

I trim them neat when they reach our side,
but his grapevines are pulling down
my neighbor's fence—suddenly visible,
his log splitter, half covered against the rain
by a plastic kiddie pool, a pickup topper,
each window cracked, that housed
a now defunct dog. Yesterday, his daughter,
newly washed out of rehab,
followed from the house her half-brother,
who has wrecked at least once every car
or truck they own, and who was screaming,
"I hate him." "No you don't," she said,
strangely quiet, almost tender,
though I've seen her fight the sheriff
all the way to his SUV.
"I appreciate the use of his truck," this boy
of twenty-three sobbed, "but I hate him."
The father tells me, when I see him,
his large hands held out, fingers spread,
"I don't know what to do with him."
His eyes won't meet mine, and I am forced
to wonder, not for the first time,
What have you done already?

"Every car I buy him," he says, "he wrecks."
Perhaps it's a message, I want to say.
Perhaps he wants something else.
But I keep it neat. "He's twenty-three.
Maybe it's time to stop buying cars."
He agrees, again, and I know
that after the next wreck, another car
will appear in the drive, and two days later,
a new dent. As we unweave the warped board

from the vines and set it best we can
on the posts, he shows me the ball-peen
in his right hand. "All I have left.
He broke the claws off all my other hammers."
We move to the next board. It is tedious.
I cut just a little. He pulls the board.
I prune a bit more.

Murder, Suicide

In formation, three dragonflies dip and glide
triangular, now a line. What I know of them
wouldn't bend a stem of grass. Still, I'll bet you
one gets left behind. All May, doves
fly in threes, by June, pairs. These things happen
everywhere. Maybe you are jogging
the newly graded road—its illusion
of level—and find the soft sand
at its edge. Not quicksand, but a step too far
and it's the ditch and all its burrs
faster than you'd think. Quicksand is
just that. Not the slow, torturous
suction that leaves a bit player's pith helmet
floating on the surface. Bowfishing for carp
spawning in the current, I aimed at riffling fins.
One step downstream, one leg sucked
below the bed, other foot still on the bar and the river
making its wish. Or maybe I'm jogging,
late summer, amid grasshopper clatter
and the dying buzz of cicadas. Then the singing,
beaded whir, nothing really like a rattle,
in the grass beside the road. I sidestep,
hackles rising, but my reaction might be
too late. So, when I hear of his death,
and hers, by her hand—his receptionist,
spared—I am surprised,
but only just. A friend says,
"I guess these things happen, even here."
I imagine they happen especially here,
and there, wherever you are now.

Trimming the Tree

Under the hawthorn, black-capped
chickadees and juncos feast
on seeds fallen from the feeder
to the snow. These are gifts.
We stand frozen, our children
holding red and green ornaments,
forgotten, as we watch,
from the bay window, the cardinal
on the feeder, the downy
at the suet. And then from the roof,
clattering through the branches,
a squirrel, in his red suit,
scatters sparrows and the rest.
They retreat to the red pine.
The cardinal, last to leave,
lights on a branch.

Winter at Forty-Two

The black Labrador's fresh prints
in this morning's snow
cross turkey tracks
caught in last week's ice,
and only time makes this
a different story.

        Onto the ice of our small pond,
        I have thrown a piece of riprap

The sky's business is mostly geese,
Canadas, snows, flashing
in the weak light, wings locked,
descending into fields of winter wheat,
meadowlarks and blackbirds
the roadside's only movement.

        that sank in yesterday's sunshine,
        almost half through,

At the bridge, a bald eagle
drives a pair of mallards
off the river.

        but last night's cold
        holds it tight, suspended
        between its two worlds, the one
        it has known since it was quarried,
        the one it is going to.

The Pilings

Thirty minutes to kill, I wander
the river west from the county bridge,
past the broken bottles, clay pigeons,
and spent shotgun shells. At my feet,
small tracks of muskrats and raccoons
who litter the river's edge
with clam shells and carp flesh.
I walk the sandbar, then the bank,
pick up the deer trail,
old as the river's current path.
I could walk all day, I suppose,
trying to find the pattern of these findings,
and not lose sight of soda cans or Styrofoam.
I turn by beaver-chewed saplings
to move back, with the river, toward the car.
Under the bridge, empty wooden crates
and a stone fire ring, each rock the size
of two fists. In the circle, crate wood,
half-burnt scantlings of lovers, or fishermen,
or those who made graffiti on the cement pilings—
one figure, erect phallus twice his size,
labeled "USA," another in front
on hands and knees labeled, "Terrorist."
Another drawing in red—a face, circles for breasts,
paint dripping from its crotch—"Love
spelled backwards is EVOL." Then the pelt.
Black. Skunk, I think, though I see no stripe,
only fur edged with sand.
A stick for a lever, I try to turn it, to identify.
Pry up instead a grin, a dark
epiphany of snout, ears, and empty sockets,
a small dog's head, unburied by wind and water,
or perhaps left unburied, under this bridge

I cross daily, where I have seen a bald eagle
drive mallards from the water,
where I watch a blue heron walk its slow edge
upstream. Perhaps even plastic, in time's fullness,
will be subsumed in the river's remaking.
It is all I have for faith.

Poem for Spring

The dog and I walk our road toward dusk,
noses clutching wood smoke
like incense to our scarred hearts.
These days we must live
with the faith of the red tail,
believing geese inking the sky
will wing north with the greening,
bringing birth and sweet death
in the grass. Weeks still we must tread
the cold Eucharist of loam, our tongues
swollen, panting for drink.

And some days, harder still this seems,
sometimes the downward spiral,
sometimes the swift descent.
But then,
        a new cardinal
singing out his lust
in the full bloom of a redbud
can rend my heart. Days like that,
I vow to stay.

Into Distant Grass

Some evenings call us to attention,
overwhelming in their bounty.
A spike buck steps from brush
sixty yards to my left. Overhead,
a lone Canada goose plies his line,
neither calling nor craning his head.
The dog and I take the left-hand road,
though it dead ends. I find the buck
where my eyes left him, whisper, "Heel,"
walking slowly, eyes down. At some point, we
cross a line. The buck canters left. Stops.
We turn, walk toward him. He returns,
and twice more we play before the dog
and I find our usual loop.
Five cattle egrets row silently
under clouds' orange bellies. Near my feet
in the grass, a dog's femur, cleaned white,
smooth in my right hand. On the hillside,
yucatilla full of pods. I think
of women, peasant blouses just
off their shoulders. Someone south
rings a dinner bell.

I deny the dog his persistent nose,
make him sit under the catalpa
until the mockingbird has run his notes
a second time. Even though at home
wait a wife and children who love me,
here, the day's last heat rises from the dust,
the cool from the field on my left
crosses my cheek, and a jay
makes his final undulating flight
before darkness. I stare into distant grass,
waiting for a vague silhouette
to move, for the next thing to show itself.

Attention

My son has discovered the atlatl.
Standing in the garden, he spears
a green tomato with a bamboo stake,
holds it overhead
and whips it.
The next he decides
will come my way, here in the hammock.
He wants it close, but if I don't move,
it will likely hit me. My two-year-old daughter
who I've just told to get down
from the crossbar between the swing set's legs
is now swinging on her belly, too far forward,
about to tumble onto her head. The black Lab,
who can jump the chain-link fence,
without a run, stands two feet from it,
hackles up, having seen the neighbor's cat.
The tomato descends. I shift,
overbalancing the hammock.

Water

Some evenings call us to attention,
just like 44 is a palindrome,
much as is a boy, seemingly forever
throwing rocks into the faintest pond
and a small girl following a smaller dog
breaking trail up a hill of clay, once
the pond, but which now looks down on
the lightest patch of rain
floating on clay under a patch of light
breaking thin clouds above a puppy
and a girl running, almost falling,
downhill to her brother, who launches
another rock, on my birthday,
into the water.

The Perfect Poem

would say only the words
sun and stone, stream and tree
and earth, yet it would explain
what I know of home
standing in the late summer's
hazy evening light, dust rising
and settling on the road,
under the smell of cottonwoods,
the last of the day's
sun on this heart-shaped
leaf in my hand.

It would say only
the words fire
and flood, wind
and grass, yet
would capture my surprise
each spring at the turning in
of the compost,
last summer's onion stalks,
cucumber skins, and grass clippings
now dirt. Stirred
in the wet heat
of last August and broken
by worms and coffin cutters,
they have all become again
that which they were,
the perfect poem.

Sighting

The first mile of my run,
at a hill's slightest rising,
two deer, one crossing, one still
on the shoulder. I stop.
Wind keeps my sound
above the breeze. The engine
of a car behind me. One hand up,
I point with the other to the does.
The car slows, four heads turn. Just
when I think they see, the driver
guns the engine. Brake lights.
A near miss. No idea
what to look for. When I pull even
with the deer's crossing,
they are gone to grass.

I cross the highway, wind
from a semi at my heels. Almost
past the field on my left, even
with its western shelterbelt, two does
and yearling fawns grazing
where spruce meets fence. I stop
beyond the trees, step slowly back
once into their sight,
a second before they flag me
with their tails, bound twenty yards,
stop. We stand, eyeing each other
until my sweat goes cold,
until I am nearly too stiff to run. I start.
They spring away. I
make my way home
in the sun's last burning.

Rain Comes Riding

Between the Fall Grass

and the fox's cry—
so like a woman screaming—
I hear the owl walk sideways on the branch
of the mugo pine
I cut down two summers past,
taken by bark beetles
and burnt that winter. Things are changing.
I can hear them in the smoke steps
of a great horned owl who flew
into the tree, not seeing
me in the screen porch, almost
asleep in the gloaming,
in the movement of beetles
I almost hear in the pine.
                              Then the fox,
one field west—its cry
frightening enough for me to cross
the road first time I heard it,
sure some neighbor or poor traveler
was meeting red death
in green summer's grass.
I watched the owl
shift himself, then let loose
his own great hoot,
as underneath him, beetles
took a better hold, and time
took its time with us.

Broken Knife at Forty-Five

The crayfish on the sandbar, where he lies
bleaching white against the tan, is of a piece
with the monarch's slow unfolding
in mid-October's tired sun. Both whisper
the open secret of my life. Here
in the gravel, strange, dubious treasures
come to rest until the change
of the next hard rain—petrified bark,
archaic bison tooth, fragment
of ossified bone, and a broken
flint knife caught in dry reeds.
Fingering its flaked edges,
I lament its maker's careless hands,
the river's torque, whatever snapped
the jasper blade neatly into halves.
I imagine its mate
on the next bar upstream.
But river is not field, where a plow
may turn up half a spearpoint and a decade later
its other half. On the river,
all our bags are packed,
or we are fools. Best to thank fate
for putting even a broken
blade in the way and tuck half a knife
into my pocket and walk again
upstream, water carrying the loosened sand
of my steps behind me. Minnows flit beyond
my trundling, and living crawdads
back into shadow.

Lightning Strike

Sometimes you curse the rain
and the footprints you find
seemingly on every sandbar,
empty of flint,
as you make your way
downriver. You imagine a man
stooping to pick from everyday gravel
the perfect arrowpoint,
the one that has waited
a thousand years for you.
You feel gray as this day,
as the water running
from the brim of your hat,
the water that ripples the shallows,
distorting the stones below,
muddying the river. Then,
rounding a bend, you see
the young buck, two tines to a side,
on the northern bluff, still,
until you look up
from the pair of red admirals
that land on your leg and chest
to find him gone.
Just a few steps downstream
and lightning
sears the sky behind
where the deer had stood
and the thunder's concussion
arrives with the flash.
You make your way upstream
to the waiting car,
every rain-beaten stone
a new struck spark.

Idyll

The dog's ashes work their way
deeper into the garden's soil.
This season I walk alone,
the dirt road winding
into darkening sky.
The horses no longer
come when called, and the wind
keens, "Winter is coming on."
The rising moon rattles the dry grass,
and below, the dead
continue their long work.

Rain Comes Riding

A day so gray wills a question.
The mule won't come to the fence
and South lies the way of all trouble.
Hands anxious in our pockets,
we bare our necks to the sky.
Rain is riding up from the panhandle.
The women sleep
                and the men
are all over themselves.
And the rain rides North like Pancho Villa.

Someone asks a question
no one answers, and night
lies far away
like a sleeper who will not rouse.
The horse whickers at the fence
waiting for an apple.
                    Jingling change
and pocket knives, and then the rain
comes riding North, letting loose with both hands.

Driving the Heart

of our country,
on a day too temperate for winter
and too beautiful to die, I watch
geese string across our southern sky
while the radio spools news: new car
bombs, polar caps melting, and west,
snow breaks a little our state's long drought.

Once a man told his story: why snakes
lack legs and why you and I
must someday die. But, he said,
until we do, we may sit at the head
of this crowded table.
Many carry that tale
to their hearts, a kind of carrion
they can eat, growing fat
but never full, hungering
for a thing they have forgotten.

Robins come early now, and geese
never leave. Our seasons milder,
we have become their south. Doves
winter in the trees behind our house.
Northward, bears swim
searching lost ice. We drive
a narrow road, leaving heavy tracks.
The clouds ride full to our west.
Let us hope for snow.

Other tales tell of naming, a duty
I have often taken to heart, learning
to call the hawks who ride
our rich winds red-tailed, Cooper's,
sharp-shinned, as if such things meant

anything. Proud I have been
to own those words.
A cardinal crosses our road,
his red a constant vaunting. The air
waves fill, our leaders' voices loud,
telling us we have everything to fear
and nothing to fret.
Heavy wind blows up from the south,
and the car pulls toward the ditch,
not wanting to be steered.

Three Views of the Deity

The kestrel breaks fast
below the lowest bough of the pear tree,
a nestling in his talons, two kingbirds in pursuit.
And behind them, a raucous jay,
trailing, waiting for a chance.

In front of sun-spoked clouds,
above the too-vivid green of the rain-beaten grass,
a cattle egret, blindingly white,
rows in silence through a patch of purest blue.

Below the cry of the kingfisher,
you walk upstream in chest-deep,
fast water, wondering at the foolishness
that led you to this chance and hoping
to make the bank, realizing that water
is the child of the lord whose mother
constantly calls it home.

On an Island in the Keys

eleven goats keep watch
around a tree house ladder.
They call, but no one answers
or comes down, no one
shows his head. Their rectangular
pupils, so much themselves
like doors, open into nothing
we can see.

Sometimes a fisherman escaping heat
wends through the palms
to their clearing. Curious
or incautious, he may start to climb.
Looking down, he will see
(their hooves noiseless in the sand)
a ring of goats staring. Then one
will raise her head, then the next,
then the bleating. Unnerved,
he may leap down amidst the "Maa-maa!"
and eyes declaring nothing.
At that moment, he will think only
of water, the sanctuary of a small boat.
He will run, goats at his thighs,
under a sky unbearably blue. Fumbling
at the knot, shoving off, wet
to the knees, the hullabaloo behind him
portentous, yet when he looks
over his shoulder, the beach
will be empty.

Over his beer, he will almost wonder
if it happened as he recalls. The day
was sultry. Perhaps he dozed. Joined

by friends, he is unsure what to say.
Sirius burning above them,
eleven heads stare one last time
up toward an empty door
before kneeling to sleep.

A Little Death

A 38-year-old Australian dentist blew his nose with such force that he expelled 60 percent of the frontal lobe of his brain through his sinuses. When paramedics arrived, Marv Tyrier of Brisbane was already dead. "This is definitely one for the books," said the editor of the medical journal Anomalous Deaths.

—The Week, 23 April 2004

I imagine so.

There is something spectacular in becoming the punch line
to a sixth-grade joke.

A friend of mine could snort a beaded chain through his soft
palate and saw back and forth, one end out his nose, the
other out his mouth—"mental floss."

Remember the public service announcement?—"A mind is a
terrible thing to waste."

Hemingway watched his crumble from booze and concussions,
long before he emptied his cranium on the walls.

George Perkins writes: "In the early morning of July 2, 1961,
standing beside his beloved gun-rack in his home, he died of
head wounds resulting from the discharge of his favorite
shotgun, in his own hands."

In history class, my sixth-grade teacher told us that during the
Terror, the executioner would grab the head from the
basket and show it its body—three minutes till brain
death—the crowd watching the face's reaction to the last
thing it saw.

Mr. Tyrier, if he could see what he'd expelled (my college
biology teacher called the sneeze the body's only other
orgasm—the little death, indeed) may not, given he'd
lobotomized himself, have recognized his dilemma, but
perhaps his last thoughts were the fascination of a toddler
looking back into the toilet.

"Lobotomized," I say and think of McMurphy—stone-faced
before the Chief gives him the pillow.

Frances Farmer, though, was the real McCoy. The "high-strung" actress, committed to an asylum where she was sold for sex, was given a lobotomy so she could live out her days, if not her life, a "calmer" woman.

Perhaps Mr. Quayle was right: "A mind is a terrible thing."

You remember standing at the urinal in that college bar and the smartass next to you saying, "You know, you're pissing away 10,000 brain cells with each ounce of alcohol."

In college, my wife's childhood friend later shot himself with his deer rifle (I have no knowledge of his feelings for it).

Dutch, my sixth-grade friend, stepped from his fiancée's VW at fifty-five miles an hour, brain trauma the cause of death. They'd been arguing. He wanted the last word.

My great-grandmother, on my father's side, died at ninety-nine—able to remember the Indians of her childhood and what the neighbor told her the day before—peacefully, in her sleep.

You remember *The Deer Hunter*? DeNiro, Walken, and Savage play Russian roulette with their VC captors who slap our boys in the face screaming the Vietnamese equivalent of "Now! Do it now!" to get them to pull the trigger.

My great-grandmother, on my mother's side, could remember bus routes around Greeley, but forgot her own son, who himself, later, needed maps in towns he'd known like the scars on his hands.

I remember the trailer I lived in with my parents in Fort Collins the first nine months of my life. My keys are a daily mystery.

But I'm fairly happy with this poem, having learned from another poet who once lived in my town to lower my standards, and who wrote on the back of a letter the day he died, "and all my love," and in a poem that same day, "You can't tell when strange things with meaning / will happen. I'm [still] here writing it down / just the way it was. 'You don't have to / prove anything,' my mother said. 'Just be ready for what God sends.'"

My mother, at sixty-two, has decided to take up the violin, having
    read some "use it or lose it" article on the brain.
I suppose, but my sense is some bastard long ago loaded the
    pistol and spun the cylinder. "Now!" he shouts, or its
    equivalent in any language. "Oh, and, all my love."

Spring And

Say what you will, these moments are my own
to arrange as I desire. Welcome.
Welcome, I say. Breathe
in this air.

A spot of blood among the white
blossoms of the Bradford pear,
a cardinal sings, "Lust"
amid the incarnadine scent,
as I muscle the tiller
across the yard into the garden
to turn into the dirt last year's grass
clippings, orange rinds, and coffee grounds,
to work in the ash of winter's fires.

I know you expect a certain thing,
that here should come a turn, self-
assured as the poem pulls the trigger
on itself, finds its final direction. These things
need time. You plant the seed in good
ground, and the sun must, and rain
must, and someone must
sit at the garden's verge playing jazz chords
on an old guitar. Corn groans
in its growing. Listen,

what's here, in my pocket? A chip
of flint. See, its edge has seen work
of hands now dirt a thousand years,
the thousand it took to work its way
up to our surface, for a tine to catch
and turn it into the sun of spring
planting. See, it is not made into a point,

or knife, not shaped to scrape a hide,
just a flake of flint with one worked edge,
for practice, maybe. Well, make of that
what you desire. We are only talking
while we plant seeds, and tune
our guitar, while an old friend
sings his many notes all made
of one word. And under us the dead
and the living exchange coats.
Above us that bird would return
all his hard-won color for the orange
beak of a mate he knows will come, if only
she can hear his call. Can you
smell it now? This moment? It is
Spring and

Under Kansas

prairie are roots
that can reach down
twelve feet—our own
Sargasso Sea
holding chipped flint,
pot sherds, sharks' teeth,
and the one thing
that can save us.

Prayer

Often there is a hill
north of your town, a place
where the sky blooms,
and below it running water,
a creek or stream, perhaps a river,
and at your feet, partway downhill,
you will find a shape,
almost like a heart,
in the rain-beaten dirt,
something familiar and unknown,
a stone, gray with blue banding,
sun-warm in your hand, its edges
worked by other hands;
its use, as you rub off the dirt
with your thumb, will come to you,
a little spit and you see it clean,
feel the click of antler flaking flint,
and now you begin anew.

One Day in Kansas

It is always disappointing to ask for gold and be given melons.

—Elliott West on Coronado

Despite their guide, they used
a sextant and ship's compass
to navigate the grass
that grazed their horses' bellies
and rose again unbent
behind armored men astride—
heavy horses, trailing cattle,
swine, and camp followers.
"We could look behind,"
they wrote, "and see nothing
of our passing across that grass."

Mexico had bent to their will
like a damp dream of youth. Here,
there were only grass and sweat,
and black flies. People fed them
then pointed further north,
until the day there was nothing left
but to strangle the man they'd shanghaied,
who had taken them where they commanded
but not where they desired. Nothing
but to return over that sea of grass,
under sky bigger than they wished
to contemplate, to the spent dreams
of the south.

Wichita: A Star Rises

Crossing the Arkansas River bridge into Delano
where cowboys find whiskey and cheer women
racing naked through the streets, Wyatt Earp stops
to watch a blue heron hunt, admiring the stealth
of its knife-walk upriver, its whistling
strike, so much like his own fists, which are his pride,
more than the pistol he wears checking chimneys
and catching dogs, duties that eclipse his day. But today
is bright, and every stairwell, doorframe, and
alleyway will be a chance, might shadow a trap. The water
is muddy, but he can sense the sureness of the bird's feet
on mossy rocks, though he cannot see Dodge
or Tombstone, where bullets comb the air
when the two sides meet like Doc's pliers
on a ragged tooth. He is young. He smiles
at his sun-backed reflection in the dark water, smooths
his big mustache with a thoughtless hand. In the Carey House,
Nell sets aside her ironing, hands him her weekly fine
and a sandhill plum, sweet in his white teeth.

I-70 West

You step from conditioned air
onto the broiling tarmac
of a gas station—Wakeeney, Oakley,
Colby, somewhere on the western
edge of Kansas—eyes straining,
desiring mountains. "Flat,"
you say, hot wind in your teeth.
Look behind you. You have risen
three thousand feet
since you left Kansas City, more
than you will climb again
by Denver. You have watched for miles
wheat and tumbleweeds.
Two pheasants—their blue-green
heads—have shown themselves.
"Kansas," you think,
but like you, they are visitors,
just passing.
"Not much to do," you say
to the attendant, who pushes your change
across the counter. He smiles,
his heart a glad riot, rejoicing
in your choice of the interstate.

Things That Are True in Our Town

This summer, 6,000 family motor coaches
found their way here.

Sometimes, even in our town, people are put into cars,
and no one sees them again.

At 23rd and Severance squats the roundabout teaching
us a new way to go straight.

The local historian tells us the British drive
the wrong side of the road because they once wanted
to keep sword hands close to passersby.

We learn Captain Cook's men, in Tahiti, traded iron for sex,
pulling nails from their ships till they nearly sank.

Part of our town blew up. Natural gas loosed its bonds, crept
along sandstone deep underground, once the floor
of an inland sea, that even now coughs up petrified teeth
of sharks larger than cars. When they breached, fires
burned for months.

In the middle of our town lolls a spaceship that never
made the moon.

What We Know

We come to this place
in the Flint Hills and begin
by naming the things we know:
big bluestem, little bluestem,
switchgrass. We indulge
a moment's satisfaction and move on:
"Red-tailed," we say, and later,
squinting against the impossibly
bright sky, "Cooper's hawk?"
Now we are less certain of
our birthright, as the cottonwoods
obscure our sight; now we are closer
to our home. We make our way,
unsure, and at our feet, everywhere,
the stone for which we have named
a place that has carried on
under other names, and none. This
is the place we want to come to, walking
in grass waxing our hands
when we roll it in our fingers,
under the smell of trees
whose heart-shaped leaves
sing up the wind,
and when the bird rises again,
soaring into the golden circle, it does so
a god. Now, we can sing
this moment, this place.

Hearing the River

There are windows that open and close like steel traps.

—William Stafford, in an interview with Steven Hind

It's a hard gentleness.
Try living
that way, minute by minute,
or even by day.
We live in the mind's
light, dreaming
fields we will never walk
but vow to,
while outside,
the current waits.
Sometimes we wake
in the dark
and know the churning
that would free us
from doubt's eddy,
a voice saying,
"It's 4 a.m. Swim."

Sonnet 1.618

Just in the way sneezewort

proves Fibonacci, so too your body
approves Duchamp, thou glowing

pentagram. Thou rectangle of whirling squares,
to watch your finger curl
like a monkey's tail . . . Your cat's claws

the logarithmic spiral of my nights.
Taking the measure of your sole
to knee, knee to navel,
undone by math, I lose myself
to the beauty of your golden section.

Seeing You Tonight, I Realized

There are deer trails undiscovered
in this wood we have walked
a hundred years that, suddenly revealed,
devour my breath. These same roads
are found in some clouds
but only by the sharpest ears,
and long must you wander there
before the slightest sound,
an echo barely heard,
gives away the secret turn,
the place the hawks' cries
grow loud in freshest air—call
and response, and then a round
you must follow, sharp-eyed,
tracing the steps in a roar
of wind sliding between trees,
like coyote over there
sniffing prints, his breath
sounds of the fire burning
in the heart of these sacred woods
where I will stay lost forever.

Satori

I follow the boy,
his head a little slow,
who has come to retrieve,
for the fifth time,
his four-hundred-pound Angus steer
who found its way again
into our yard, and now
walks behind the boy,
following the feed bucket
in the hand that keeps it
to the ditch side of the road.
I carry the boy's Welsh Corgi,
his "cow dog,"
who would not follow when called
and smells
like the carpet of a roadhouse,
as lightning
frames our night and headlights
turn the dog's head into my neck,
and I know
I can walk, following this slow boy,
this young steer, carrying this foul,
sweet dog, its head under my chin,
as long as I need.

Thin Ice

He wakes in blue neon snow
under the factory lights, wakes
from the warm whispers
of his dreams. Maybe he'll lose
only pieces of his cheek, the tip
of his nose. The river
is scabbed with ice. There was
a time his face was smooth, the rink
before the first skate, his dreams
a stream moving forward. They are
a pond now, too small
to turn over with the seasons,
but it is summer there. Frogs
are calling from the sedge.
Now, he finds his legs. Sees
the Schlitz Light,
a small fire in the distance,
a place to warm his hands. Walks
as if the world might not
hold his weight.

Deadman

1.

Deadman lays out a spread
for all his friends
who come, eyes or no,
to see him.
Those without,
shall nose him,
rich repast,
capon of dark mystery.
Such tales he could tell
of life forgotten,
remembered in his cells
and in those
who rode along.
He would be toastmaster
extraordinaire had dirt
not stopped his expression.
And he would speak of dreams,
if he could only wake.
Peace, Deadman, rest.
Take this morsel
of time, a strange stray
bays far away. Patience,
he will be here soon.

2.

Deadman, a little stiff, lies
almost awake,
dreaming, in faint iambics,
of mermaids. Uncertain pressure
informs his sleep, dreams of deep
water, locked vaults, diminished
oxygen. Even the sky of his mind
oppresses. He wonders through his world
breaking down. If only he could wake,
but his eyes are weighted
as with copper,
and what his sleeping ears hear
troubles him. Sounds of crawling,
gnawing, and most troublesome
of all—a continuous seepage.
He is thankful for the mermaids,
and their songs, even if, as he now
thinks, the songs are not for him.
Enough to lie here listening, his collar
high and tight. But then
a new sound, someone howling
through blankets of earth. And what
is that? Scratching?

3.

A dog whines at the door. Deadman
wonders should he be the one
to open it, worries that doing
so breaks some protocol.
The attendant scratching
he finds grating,
here, supine, half-sleeping.
Surely someone will shoo the dog,
or welcome it. Why must he, stirred
from rich dreams (or so he senses them),
be the one? "Thus was it
ever," he thinks. "No, I'll not
be bothered, scratch and whine as you will.
I'll return to the gold and pink,
silver and green of dreams."
Then light
licks his face, snuffling
in his ears, and above the hullaballoo,
he swears he hears birdsong.
As his eyes begin to adjust to this new
brightness, he says—says indeed—"Well,
this is unexpected."

4.

Deadman steps from the dirt.
In truth, steps is too dramatic.
He hitches to his side, rolls to his
forehead, pushes to his knees—
a great creaking—rises in waspy
jerks. Stands, stretches, looks
around, ignoring the raking light,
the nine-call run of the mockingbird,
the leaves hollering full summer,
and is put off by the lack of witnesses.
Surely this great feat, pulled off
with no more intervention
than the pawing of a cur
must have witnesses.
Who will believe him? No fear,
my friend. Flies are gathering,
and vultures, your guidons. Green
now as Lazarus in your new situation,
you will grow tired of your celebrity.
Brush away the dirt. Bid your close
friends feed elsewhere. Look again.
It is the old world, not a next,
and it is deep, rich summer,
and you are   something.
Try out those walkers, old sport.
Spit the dirt from your words.
This is Christmas in July,
or Easter. What will you do
with the present? Your gait
is rusty and swings hiccuppingly
along, but you are moving
the right way (there
seems no wrong) to town. Direction
will find you, or not.
You are like us now, Deadman.
Purpose is assured only in the ground.

29.

Deadman writes his first song,
music and lyrics.
It is of water passing
through and by as one lies
alone embraced by soil.
It is a train song, a lover leaving
song, that the living do not get,
though they love his voice,
and the band plays like hell.
It is a dilemma.
                    He is flattered
by their adulation.
He loves their loving him.
But something has changed. He needs
a deeper connection. It is an old
story, one without a happy ending,
but endings seem irrelevant
to Deadman. All he can do
is write (trite, he thinks).
Finally, he has come to understand.
He writes another song about water,
tries to get it right.

30.

Deadman walking
a gravel bar by the river
discreetly wondering
about throwing himself in,
comes upon the perfect
bottle for a slide—
green glass, a little longer
than his middle finger,
raised letters:
"Mrs. Winslow's Soothing Syrup."
Without wondering why,
he bites a little below
the bottle's neck,
spins it in his mouth,
spits out the bottle's neck,
a neat trick,
one he wishes he'd have had
at the freak show.
It now fits perfectly
his long ring finger.
No more taloned grip
on a whole bottle.
He'll throw himself in
tomorrow, drown
or find the delta.
Today, he wants to know
Mrs. Winslow.
Google and the lead guitarist
phone-summon her ghost:
teething drops from the late
1800s, their main ingredient,
morphine, a favorite
of soldiers home

from the Civil War.
"Baby Killer," it was called.
One ad shows a mother
in white gown
touching her baby's teeth,
like God touching Adam
in Michelangelo's
mediocre ceiling.
Deadman could sleep,
really sleep. Maybe
morphine, or heroin,
also found in teething drops,
his guitarist says. The image
of his living mother is less
clear than that of Mrs. Winslow.
Adam though he is, he knows
no god. No one
told him get up
and walk, to throw off
the clothes of the grave.
Even the dog who raised him
is dead. He plays
the slide on the Gibson
hollow-body.
What is rendered
is the truest blues,
rivers roiling, and homes
never returned to.

31.

Deadman writes the perfect song
on a popsicle wrapper tumbled
down the street at just the moment
of his inspiration. The song
captures everything he knows,
feels about being alive
                        after being dead.
It is a perfect blues. He folds
the sticky wrapper, carries it
in his palm, a kind of grail, home
to the Fender Nocaster
and the green glass slide.
Finger in the slide, the slide
just touching the strings, the tubes
in the tweed Fender Champ
warming, his head
in a minor key, Deadman knows
this is going to be good.
                        He opens his mouth
at the amplifier's hum and begins
to bawl. There are no tears,
just dry wracking sobs. It is hours
before they subside. He has leaned
too close to the amp.
Its humming calls him back.
He switches it off, racks
the ancient Fender.
By the last light of the day, filtered
through the blinds, he pulls a small
framed photo off the studio wall,
removes the picture of himself
and the original Deadman Band,
replaces it with the wrapper, rehangs
the frame on the wall. The world
will have to wait.

34.

Deadman has had enough
of fame, of groupies, of being
the only true dead man walking.
Even his art seems not enough.
Tired of his own voice, and finally
even of the slide moving up the strings,
Deadman would have an end to it.
Always before, that bobber, hope,
had popped back up, and Deadman
had found reason to move on. Now,
though, is enough. A big fish
pulls the bobber. It will not rise.
Deadman has found real purpose:
how to make an end. Peace,
Deadman, old friend. Enjoy
the river rolling on your right,
the sunshine on this day under a sky
so large it seems a question. Those
who can help are on their way.
Together they are not afraid,
and all of them are hungry.

35.

Deadman ends ignobly, some would say,
not so Deadman. Reborn of canine attention,
what better way to leave than at the teeth
of a pack of feral strays, acting upon our basest
need. Slim pickings, Deadman thinks, and laughs,
coming undone, feeling little of what we
would call pain, but, surprisingly, a bit of longing
for things not done. For the curs,
it is like devouring cotton candy,
dry morsels disappearing almost the instant
they enter their mouths, even his bones
unsatisfactory, until all that remains
is laughter in the empty sky
as they stalk for shadows, like us
unsated by repast.

About the Author

William Sheldon lives in Hutchinson, Kansas. He is the author of three other books of poetry, *Retrieving Old Bones* (Woodley Press, 2002), *Rain Comes Riding* (Mammoth Publications, 2011), *Deadman* (Spartan Press, 2021), as well as a chapbook, *Into Distant Grass* (Oil Hill Press, 2009). He plays bass for the bands The Excuses and Cow Creek Blues.

Acknowledgments

Many thanks to the editors of the following, where these poems appeared, sometimes in slightly different forms:

Coal City Review: "Lying on the Lawn"

The Coop: A Poetry Cooperative: "River Sartoris," "Smoke in the Distance," "Thrall," "Three Rivers," "Time," "What I Know Today," "The World and Oysters"

Flint Hills Review: "Benediction," "Smoke in the Distance," "When I Go West"

HomeWords: "This House" (from "Body House Land Sky")

Hutchinson Magazine: "Right Now: Arkansas River," "Small Bill of Rights," "Through Difficulty"

I-70 Review: "After All," "Caught," "Open Window," "Low," "Our Present Sky," "Our Son is Leaving," "Palimpsest," "What We Write About" (under the title "Love and the Absence Of Love")

Konza: A Bioregional Journal: "Ungrassed, the Land," "With the Low Poppy Mallow"

150 Kansas Poems: "Birdseed," "Hunting Arrowheads on the Arkansas"

Slant: "Matins," "The Strange Promise of Fall"

"A Better Heaven," "Funereal," and "I'd Like to Be There" appeared in the anthology *The Gasconade Review Presents: Strange Gods of the Prairie* (Spartan Press, 2021).

"Helping the Needy," "This World, Not the Next," and "Yes, I Said Perfect" appeared in the anthology *Bards Against Hunger: Kansas* (Local Gems Press, 2018).

"Ad Astra Per Aspera" appeared in the anthology *To the Stars Through Difficulties: A Kansas Renga in 150 Voices* (Mammoth Publications, 2012).

Selected poems are from the following collections:

Retrieving Old Bones, Woodley Press, 2002.

Into Distant Grass (Oil Hill Press, 2009). (Most of the poems in *Into Distant Grass* first appeared as an internal chapbook in *The Midwest Quarterly*, vol. 49, no. 4, 2008).

Rain Comes Riding, Mammoth Publications, 2011.

Deadman, Spartan Press, 2021.

Gratitude

I would like to thank Tracy Million Simmons, my publisher and book designer, Linzi Garcia, my conscientious and thorough editor, and Natalie Wolf, editorial intern at Meadowlark Press. I couldn't have asked for better folks to work with. Many thanks as well to Stephen Meats, John Jenkinson, Denise Low, and Jason Ryberg, editors of the selected works that appear here. I also owe a great debt to Steven Hind and Harley Elliott for their insightful and honest criticism over the years, and especially for their friendship. Thanks to Scott Brown, a good man to ride the river with, for the cover photo, and long friendship. Thank you to Hutchinson Community College and the Fine Arts and Humanities Department for the sabbatical that allowed me to complete this book. And finally, thanks to my wife Cindy, well, for everything.

Meadowlark POETRY

Books are a way to explore, connect, and discover. Poetry invites us to observe and think in new ways, bridging our understanding of the world with our artistic need to interact with, shape, and share it with others.

Publishing poetry is our way of saying:
We love these words,
we want to preserve them,
we want to play a role in sharing them
with the world.

Follow Meadowlark Press
on Facebook & Instagram

(f) facebook.com/ReadAMeadowlarkBook

(O) @meadowlarkbooks